MAKER
KIDS

W9-AOS-866

High-Tech
DIY Projects
with
Electronics, Sensors, and LEDs

Maggie Murphy

PowerKiDS press

New York

Published in 2015 by The Rosen Publishing Group, Inc.
29 East 21st Street, New York, NY 10010

First Edition

Editors: Jennifer Way and Jacob Seifert
Book Design: Andrew Povolny
Photo Research: Katie Stryker

Photo Credits: Cover Thomas Trutschel/Photothek/Getty Images; p. 4 Steve Cukrov/Shutterstock.com; p. 5 Jason Vandehey/Shutterstock.com; p. 6 Heike Brauer/iStock/Thinkstock; p. 7 Dan Dalton/Caiaimage/Getty Images; p. 9 (top) Joseph O. Holmes/Moment/Getty Images; p. 9 (bottom) Carl Iwasaki/Time & Life Pictures/Getty Images; p. 10 Image Source/Photodisc/Thinkstock; p. 11 akdemirhk/iStock/Thinkstock; p. 12 Dario Sabljak/Shutterstock.com; p. 13 (top) Staras/iStock/Thinkstock; p. 13 (bottom) Marco Hegner/iStock/Thinkstock; p. 14 monkeybusinessimages/iStock/Thinkstock; p. 15 Jupiterimages/Stockbyte/Thinkstock; pp. 16, 18–21, 23–25 Katie Stryker; p. 17 Krasowit/Shutterstock.com; p. 22 c.d. stone; p.25 © Arduino; p. 26 Edyta Blaszczyk/Odessa American/APimages; p. 27 Singkham/Shutterstock.com; p. 28 Huntstock/Vetta/Getty Images; p. 29 Mettus/Shutterstock.com.
Project Credit: pp. 24–25 code courtsey of John Edgar Park of Jpixl.net.

Library of Congress Cataloging-in-Publication Data

Murphy, Maggie, author.
 High-tech DIY projects with electronics, sensors, and LEDs / by Maggie Murphy. — First edition.
    pages cm. — (Maker kids)
 Includes index.
 ISBN 978-1-4777-6672-9 (library binding) — ISBN 978-1-4777-6678-1 (pbk.) —
 ISBN 978-1-4777-6659-0 (6-pack)
 1. Electronics—Juvenile literature. 2. Electronic apparatus and appliances—Design and construction—Juvenile literature. 3. Detectors—Design and construction—Juvenile literature. 4. Light emitting diodes—Juvenile literature. I. Title. II. Title: High-tech do-it-yourself projects with electronics, sensors, and LEDs.
 TK7820.M87 2015
 621.381—dc23
                                     2014002117

Manufactured in the United States of America

CPSIA Compliance Information: Batch #WS14PK9: For Further Information contact Rosen Publishing, New York, New York at 1-800-237-9932

Contents

Be a Maker!

You use electronic **devices** every day, but do you know how they work? It is fun and easy to experiment with building electronic devices! Join other kids around the world in the maker movement by learning to build high-tech projects yourself.

A thermostat is an example of a sensor. It works quietly in the background to keep the temperature comfortable.

Heat
Setting
68°

9:25 AM

Inside
70°

| System | Fan | Schedule |
| Heat | Auto | |

In many electronics projects, an LED will light up when a sensor has sensed something such as movement, pressure, or sound.

Two common **components** in electronics are light-emitting diodes (LEDs) and sensors. LEDs are a type of diode. Diodes are devices that let electricity flow through them in only one direction. When connected to an electrical current, or flow of **electrons**, an LED will emit, or give off, light. A sensor is a device that **detects** or measures conditions like light, heat, or touch. In this book, you will find step-by-step directions for DIY, or do-it-yourself, electronics projects with LEDs and sensors.

Then and Now

The idea for sensors in electronics came from nature. Plants and animals have many sensors that let them detect and respond to conditions around them. For example, human eyes work as light and motion sensors.

Sensors have also been used in **engineering** for thousands of years. An example of an early sensor is the float valve in a flush toilet. The float valve floats on top of the water in the water tank. When the water in the tank is let out, the float valve lowers with the water. This opens a pipe that refills the tank. As the water rises, so will the float valve. When the tank is full, the float valve rises all the way and pinches off the water flow.

Galileo invented this thermometer in the 1600s. It uses different glass bubbles to show the temperature. It is a kind of sensor.

Many new TVs use LEDs to light their screens. LED TVs have sharper images and a wider range of colors than TVs that came before.

Modern sensors are electronic components that play an important part in interactive devices. You can find sensors in home appliances, cars, computers, and robots. Almost every device that uses a **microcontroller**, a type of small computer, to perform a certain action has a sensor for **input**.

Scientists started experimenting with light-emitting diodes in the 1920s. Red LEDs were first used in electronics in the early 1960s. Today, you can find LEDs of every color in electronic devices. For example, they are used to form numbers in digital clocks, light up traffic signals, and tell you when your home appliances are turned on. **Infrared** LEDs give off invisible light and are used to transmit information from remote controls.

LEDs are used in DIY electronics as well. An LED can be used as a simple **output** device to show that a **circuit** or a code is working.

Experimenting with Radio

Today, many people experiment with DIY electronics projects that use sensors, microcontrollers, and LEDs. In the twentieth century, many important innovations were made by people who experimented with radio technology. In fact, radio experimenters made discoveries that helped lead to the invention of television broadcasting and cellular networks.

For decades, people of all ages have enjoyed building and tinkering with electronics in their basements and garages.

How Do Sensors Work?

Sensors are what make many electronic devices interactive. A sensor will detect or measure a specific condition in the device's physical environment. The information the sensor collects about the condition is called input. The input is sent to the device's processor, which is a type of computer. Once the signal is processed, the device responds with an action, called output.

Many doors that open on their own use motion sensors. The motion they detect is the input. The doors sliding or swinging open is the output.

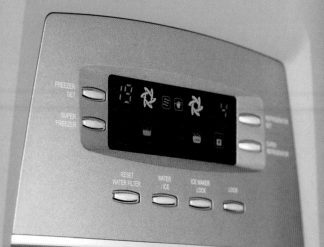

The icemaker in this refrigerator uses a sensor to tell it when to make more ice.

Infrared Sensors

Infrared sensors detect infrared light, which is not visible to human eyes. A television uses an infrared sensor to receive input from a remote control. When you press a button on a remote control, an infrared LED at the end of the control flashes a signal for the sensor to detect.

Different kinds of sensors measure different conditions. These might include heat, sound, pressure, movement, and light. Some sensors detect things people can't see, such as radiation or infrared light.

How Do LEDs Work?

Conductivity is how well something allows electricity to pass through it. Conductors have high conductivity. Many metals, like copper, are conductors. Rubber and glass are insulators. They do not let electricity pass through them at all. The diodes in LEDs are made of materials with different levels of conductivity. It is the flow of electricity through the different materials in the LED that make it light up.

LEDs have two metal legs, called leads. One is slightly longer than the other. The longer leg is the anode lead. It connects to the positive side of a power supply, such as a battery. The shorter leg is the cathode lead. It connects to the negative side of a power supply.

If you connect the cathode (shorter) lead to a positive current, the LED will not light up. This is because electricity can flow through LEDs in only one direction.

More and more people are using LED lightbulbs, like this one. They are environmentally friendly because they use little energy and last a long time.

An LED's color depends on the kind of materials the diode uses. That's why LEDs that look clear might give off colored light instead of white light.

Join a Club!

Do you like working on projects and sharing your ideas with others? Do you want to learn more about electronics projects with LEDs and sensors? If so, you should join a club! Clubs are made up of people who all share an interest. Your school may have an electronics or robotics club, or there might be one in your city or town. If not, you can ask a teacher or librarian about starting one.

Starting a club takes a lot of work. Ask a teacher to help you get supplies, find a space to hold meetings, and spread the word to others.

Have an adult help you search the Internet to see if there is already an electronics club at a school, library, community center, or business near you.

Your school might also have an electronics or robotics team. Teams take part in competitions. For example, robotics teams compete against other teams to build robots that can solve different problems.

Make an LED Throwie!

A fun project you can make to start experimenting with LEDs is an LED throwie. An LED throwie lights up and sticks to metal surfaces when it is tossed against them.

Rare-earth magnet

Electrical tape

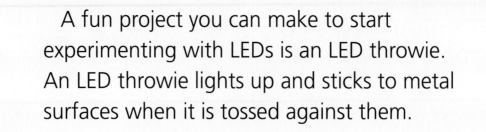

CR2032 3-volt lithium battery

10 mm diffused LED

Finding Materials

Many pharmacies, grocery stores, and retail stores carry lithium watch batteries. You can find LEDs and strong rare-earth magnets at hobby stores and retail chains such as RadioShack. If you can't find any of these supplies nearby, ask an adult to help you order them online. There are many online stores, such as Adafruit.com and Amazon.com, that sell all of these supplies.

When making LED throwies, try using different colors of LEDs.

You can be very creative with LED throwies. Check out Makezine.com/projects/extreme-led-throwies to see a bunch of different ways people have used them. What other ways can you think of to use your LED throwies?

Steps for Making an LED Throwie

You will need:

- 1 10 mm diffused LED (any color)
- 1 CR2032 3-volt battery
- 1 Rare-earth magnet
- Electrical tape

1

2

Put the lithium battery between the leads of the LED so that the anode (longer) lead is on the side of the battery's positive (+) **terminal**, or side, and the cathode (shorter) lead is on the side of the negative (-) terminal.

Wrap a piece of tape several times around the LED leads and battery, making sure the leads pinch the battery and stay in place.

Place the disc magnet against the taped-up bundle on the side of the battery's positive terminal. Wrap more tape around it to attach the magnet to the battery and LED.

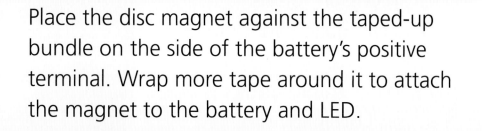

This is a finished LED throwie stuck to a computer monitor. See what else you can make your LED throwies stick to, inside and outside your home!

You've made an LED throwie!

Getting Started with Sensors

Sensors take input and send it to an electronic device's processor. To see how this works, you can build your own interactive electronic device! It is fun and easy to start building electronics projects with sensors. You can find many projects with sensors at Makezine.com and Instructables.com.

If you want to build an electronic device, you need to gather materials. There may be a nearby RadioShack, Fry's, or hobby store that carries what you will need. If you can't find something at a store, you can have an adult help you shop for it online. Makershed.com, Hobbyengineering.com, and Allelectronics.com all sell many sensors, parts, and starter kits.

This is a passive infrared (PIR) motion sensor. It detects changes in the infrared light in the area around itself.

You will also need a microcontroller board to process information from your sensors. The Arduino™ Uno is a simple microcontroller that is easy to program and use. One great thing about the Arduino™ Uno is that the software you need to program it is free!

Breadboards are used in many electronics projects. Their nodes, or strips of holes, connect components into circuits.

Soldering

Many electronic devices are made with components that are soldered together. Solder is metal that quickly melts and cools to join components. To solder something, you need a soldering iron and a coil of solder. You also need an adult to help you!

Jumper wires are used in many projects. Use different colors to help you remember which components are connected together.

Once you have your components, your next job is to connect them. Connecting components makes a circuit, or pathway for electricity. One easy way to make a circuit is to use a breadboard. A breadboard is a plastic board with many holes where you can plug in components. Breadboards test out the connections in an electronic circuit quickly and easily without soldering. If something in your project doesn't work, you can take it apart and try again. In the next chapter, you will find a step-by-step project that uses an Arduino™ Uno, a sensor, an LED, and a breadboard to build a motion-sensing alarm!

Motion-Sensing Alarm

Have an adult help you download the Arduino™ software to a computer by going to Arduino.cc and clicking on Download. The code for this project, found at the link in the materials list, is by John Edgar Park of Jpixl.net.

You will need:

- 1 Arduino™ Uno microcontroller
- 1 PIR motion sensor
- 1 buzzer
- 1 solderless breadboard
- 1 5 mm LED (color of your choice)
- 3 male/male (m/m) and 5 male/female (m/f) jumper wires
- Code from Raw.github.com /jedgarpark/Make_PIR_Sensor /master/MAKE_PIR_Sensor.pde

1

Use three m/m jumper wires to connect the pins on the Arduino™ Uno to the rows on the breadboard. Connect digital pin 2 to row 1, the 5V pin to row 3, and a GND (ground) pin to row 5.

2

If the PIR motion sensor does not have wires already connected to it, use 3 m/f jumper wires to connect its pins to the breadboard rows. Connect the OUT pin to row 1, the VCC (+) pin to row 3, and the GND (-) pin to row 5.

3

Plug the LED into the Arduino™ Uno. Plug the anode (longer) lead into digital pin 13 and the cathode (shorter) lead into the GND pin.

4

If the buzzer does not have wires already connected to it, use two m/f jumper wires. Connect the buzzer's wires to digital pin 10 and an open GND pin on the Arduino™ Uno. It does not matter which wire is connected to which pin.

5

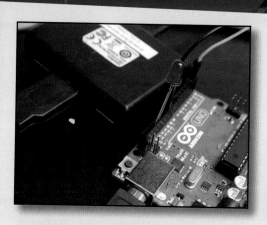

Start the Arduino™ software and connect the Arduino™ Uno to the computer with a USB cable.

6

Follow the link in the supplies list to find the code. Copy and paste it into the Arduino™ software. Upload it to the Arduino™ Uno.

7

Leave the room or stay very still for a few moments so the alarm can set itself. When the sensor detects your movement, the buzzer will go off and the LED will light up!

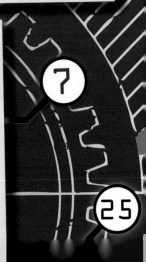

Even More Projects

You can find many electronics projects with LEDs and sensors on the Internet. The next few paragraphs describe a few really cool ones. Use the Projects Links box in this chapter to find online tutorials for each project.

If you're interested in the weather or atmosphere, check out the photometer at Makezine.com. It can detect light and even the level of water vapor in the atmosphere.

Many kids share their projects online. You can do their projects or even post your own. Often, you can leave comments about projects or ask for advice.

There are many websites that sell electronics project kits. They come with instructions and all the parts you need.

YouTube.com has an electrifying video tutorial that shows you how to make a cube out of LEDs. The coolest part is that you can program it to light up in all sorts of fun patterns!

The next two projects come from Instructables.com, a site with step-by-step directions for all kinds of DIY projects. One project teaches users how to make a temperature-sensing device that uses an LED as output. Another project helps you build a simple touch sensor that uses your finger to complete its circuit.

Projects Links

Photometer – Makezine.com/projects/build-an-led-photometer
LED Cube – Youtube.com/watch?v=IFDcdN47V5s
Temperature Sensor – Instructables.com/id/Temperature-Sensor-with-LED
Touch Sensor – Instructables.com/id/touch-sensor-LED

Keep Experimenting

The projects in this book are just the beginning of what you can do with LEDs and sensors! Once you learn the basics, try experimenting with designing your own electronic devices. You can learn everything you need to know about DIY electronics from the books, magazines, and websites listed in the next chapter.

Doing electronics experiments with someone else can be a lot of fun. You can help each other learn and share the excitement and success.

Don't be discouraged if your project doesn't work the first time. Figure out what went wrong and try a different way. It's the best way to learn.

When you build high-tech DIY projects, you are joining others in the maker movement. Try connecting with other makers online, at local maker events, or by joining an electronics club or team. Keep experimenting, and you will make something great!

More About Making

Check out the lists below for more ways to learn about electronics, sensors, and LEDs. You can also ask an adult to help you use the library and search the Internet for other projects, books, and stores!

Books

Iannini, Bob. *Electronic Gadgets for the Evil Genius: 28 Build-It-Yourself Projects*. New York: McGraw-Hill/TAB Electronics, 2004.

Platt, Charles. *Make: Electronics*. Sebastopol, CA: Maker Media, 2009.

Platt, Charles. *Make: More Electronics*. Sebastopol, CA: Maker Media, 2014.

Websites

- Find free Arduino™ software, codes, and tips at Arduino.cc.
- For electronics projects, visit Sylviashow.com.
- Complete challenges and earn a patch at Diy.org/skills/hardwarehacker.
- Find a massive online electronics community at Makezine.com.

Parts and Kits

Makershed.com
Sparkfun.com
Browndoggadgets.com